W9-AVA-685

Pebble Bilingual Books

Soy cooperativa/ I Am Cooperative

de/by
Sarah L. Schuette

Traducción/Translation
Martín Luis Guzmán Ferrer, Ph.D.

Capstone Press
Mankato, Minnesota

Pebble Bilingual Books are published by Capstone Press
151 Good Counsel Drive, P.O. Box 669, Mankato, Minnesota 56002
http://www.capstone-press.com

Printed in the United States of America

1 2 3 4 5 6 08 07 06 05 04 03

Library of Congress Cataloging-in-Publication Data
Schuette, Sarah L., 1976–
[I am cooperative. Spanish & English]
Soy cooperativa / de Sarah L. Schuette; traducción, Martín Luis Guzmán Ferrer = I am cooperative / by Sarah L. Schuette; translation, Martín Luis Guzmán Ferrer.
p. cm.—(Pebble bilingual books)
Spanish and English.
Includes index.
Summary: Simple text and photographs show various ways children can be cooperative.
ISBN 0-7368-2302-6
1. Cooperativeness—Juvenile literature. [1. Cooperativeness. 2. Spanish language materials—Bilingual.] I. Title: I am cooperative. II. Title. III. Series: Pebble bilingual books.
BJ1533.C74S3418 2004
179′.9—dc21 2003004926

Credits
Mari C. Schuh and Martha E. H. Rustad, editors; Jennifer Schonborn, series designer and illustrator; Patrick Dentinger, cover production designer; Gary Sundermeyer, photographer; Nancy White, photo stylist; Karen Risch, product planning editor; Eida Del Risco, Spanish copy editor; Gail Saunders-Smith, consulting editor; Madonna Murphy, Ph.D., Professor of Education, University of St. Francis, Joliet, Illinois, author of *Character Education in America's Blue Ribbon Schools*, consultant

Pebble Books thanks the Murphy and Polanek families of Chicago, Illinois, for modeling in this book and Rebecca Glaser of Mankato, Minnesota, for providing photo shoot locations. The author dedicates this book to the memory of her grandparents, Willmar and Janet Schuette.

Table of Contents

Contenido

I am cooperative. I work with other people.

Yo soy una persona cooperativa. Sé trabajar con los demás.

I cooperate with my family. I help my grandparents with their puzzle.

Coopero con mi familia. Ayudo a mis abuelos con sus rompecabezas.

I help my sister clean.

Ayudo a mi hermana con la limpieza.

I help set the table before meals.

Ayudo a poner la mesa antes de las comidas.

Top Dog
Things I Like To Do
My Favorite Foods
U.S. POLO ASSOC.
FOOTBALL
Caleb

I cooperate at school.
I push in my chair.

Coopero en la escuela.
Coloco mi silla
en su lugar.

Author

I help my teacher
hand out paper
when she asks.

Ayudo a mi maestra
a repartir los papeles
cuando ella me lo pide.

Today's Helpers
March
March Weather
March 6
March
Today is
A Big Happy Birthday Wish to
from Our Gang!
MY CLASS IS
100
10
Sun.
Mon.
Tues.
Wed.
Thurs.

I work with my friend
on our art project.

Trabajo con mi amigo en
nuestro proyecto de arte.

HAPPY BIRTHDAY!
January
February
April
May
June
July
August
October
November
December

I work with others on a team.

Trabajo con los demás en equipo.

CHEVROLET

I am cooperative.
I do my part.

Yo soy cooperativa.
Cumplo con mi parte.

Glossary

cooperate—to work with others and to follow rules

follow—to obey; cooperative people follow the rules at home, at school, and in their community without complaining.

help—to assist others; helpful people are cooperative when they volunteer to help someone else.

part—a share of the responsibility for something; doing your part means doing your job.

project—a school assignment that students work on over a period of time

team—a group of people who work together on a project or play a sport together

Glosario

cooperar—trabajar con los demás y cumplir con las reglas

cumplir—obedecer; las personas cooperativas cumplen las reglas en el hogar, la escuela y su comunidad sin quejarse.

ayudar—prestar cooperación a los demás; las personas que prestan ayuda cooperan voluntariamente con los demás.

parte *(la)*—una porción de la responsabilidad en algo; cumplir con tu parte significa hacer tu trabajo.

proyecto *(el)*—una tarea escolar en la que los alumnos trabajan durante un lapso de tiempo

equipo *(el)*—un grupo de personas que trabajan juntas en un proyecto o en un deporte

Index

Índice